A2 Media Studies
UNIT 5

AQA

Module 5:
Independent Study

David Probert

Philip Allan Updates
Market Place
Deddington
Oxfordshire
OX15 0SE

Tel: 01869 338652
Fax: 01869 337590
e-mail: sales@philipallan.co.uk
www.philipallan.co.uk

ISBN 0 86003 931 5

This guide has been written specifically to support students preparing for the
AQA A2 Media Studies Unit 5 examination. The content has been neither
approved nor endorsed by AQA and remains the sole responsibility of the author.
All extracts from student work have been selected and adapted to illustrate
assessment principles and marking criteria and in some cases marks awarded
in the Guide may not reflect the actual final mark achieved by the candidate.

Printed by Information Press, Eynsham, Oxford

Contents

Introduction

■ ■ ■

Content Guidance

■ ■ ■

Assessment and Examples

Introduction

About this guide

This unit guide is for students following the AQA A2 Media Studies course. It deals with Module 5, the **Independent Study**, which gives you the opportunity to pursue a research topic of your choice and produce an original study of 3,000 words supported by a bibliography. There are three sections to this guide:

- **Introduction** — this gives advice on how to use the guide, an explanation of the skills required in A2 Media Studies and how the marks are awarded, and suggestions for effective preparation and research methodologies. It concludes with a checklist for the final coursework submission.
- **Content Guidance** — this is designed to make you aware of what you need to know before undertaking the Independent Study. Advice on choice of topic and choice of title is provided. Research methods are explained and you are advised on how you should set about your research and what the best and most appropriate sources and methods are. There is also advice on how to select and edit from your research to fulfil the requirements of the specification.
- **Assessment and Examples** — this uses examples of students' work to demonstrate good practice. Grading and assessment of specific examples of Independent Studies are accompanied by examiners' comments.

How to use the guide

To make the best use of this guide in planning and completing your Independent Study, you should read it all, taking particular note of the examples of good and bad practice. Consider the range of topics available to you and look at the key ingredients of a successful piece of work. Spend some time jotting down possible study topics which interest you and ask yourself how you might formulate a question and organise a research project.

The completed study should be 3,000 words long, but this does not include all the notes, research and preparation you will need to do in order to achieve a high standard in the final submission. You should ensure that you are thoroughly familiar with the marking scheme and the Assessment Objectives before undertaking the task. Your teacher will explain how the Independent Study is to be managed in your own school or college, including deadlines for drafts and the finished piece. Discuss your title/question/hypothesis and your first rough draft with your teacher before you attempt to write up the final submission.

Look at the examples and commentaries on style and content, and when you start writing try to make sure that you follow the best practice. Learn to check and correct your work as you go along. You could try reading out passages to parents or friends to see whether what you have written makes sense.

Note: films that have an 18 certificate have been identified with an asterisk. The AQA Media Studies specification allows the use of 18-certified films. However, if you choose an 18-certified film for your Independent Study, you should discuss your choice with your teacher before commencing your written analysis.

The A2 specification

The A2 Media Studies Independent Study is designed to give you the opportunity to apply the understanding of the Key Concepts you learned at AS either to a contemporary media text or texts or to a topic or issue arising out of one or more texts. It is a text-based investigation in which you seek to explain or clarify an issue or to answer a question you have set yourself by analysing a specific, contemporary media text or texts. All the modules are interrelated and your previous work will be useful in developing your study, but Module 5 is particularly related to work done in Module 4, where, for example, genre and representation studies might lead you directly towards a Module 5 topic.

Examinable skills

There are three examinable skills in the specification, often referred to as Assessment Objectives (each counts for a percentage of the available marks):

- **Assessment Objective 1** (AO1, $2\frac{1}{2}$%) requires you to demonstrate your knowledge and application of the Key Concepts employed within Media Studies and show your use of these in evaluating texts and ideas in your study.
- **Assessment Objective 2** (AO2, $2\frac{1}{2}$%) covers your ability to demonstrate your knowledge and understanding of the wider historical, social, political and economic contexts relevant to Media Studies.
- **Assessment Objective 5** (AO5, 15%) is concerned with your ability to use appropriate investigative and research techniques in carrying out your study of a media topic. It is important that you adopt a questioning attitude to your material. You are in the role of investigator and should get used to asking yourself questions such as, 'Why was this media product made?', 'When and where was it produced or written?', 'Who were the audience members?' and 'What was the intended outcome in terms of audience response?'

The evidence from examiners indicates that a successful study should have a clearly focused and directed title — usually in the form of a question. Badly conceived titles or open-ended questions are unlikely to help you to direct your thoughts effectively. Always remember that the study is text based and indicating the text(s) you intend to study in your title is an obvious way to keep yourself on track.

The principal moderator's report on the AQA 2002 examination says on the subject of titles:

The most successful work generally centred on more focused and clearly defined titles or hypotheses, for example: 'To what extent has the representation of women changed in the James Bond series, with particular reference to *Dr No* (1962) and *The World is not Enough* (1999)?', 'To what extent do representations of women in men's lifestyle magazines such as *Loaded*, *FHM* and *Maxim* borrow from the conventions of *Playboy* and other soft-porn titles?', 'What do the contemporary films *American Beauty** (1999) and *Fight Club** (1999) tell us about the changing role of men in contemporary American society?', 'Do musical lyricists such as Marilyn Manson and Eminem use media controversy to market themselves?' or 'Within *Fight Club* does David Finch represent the values and ideology of a capitalist society as something impossible to escape?' Titles such as these pose a question and thus enable candidates to reach identifiable conclusions. Weaker work tended to be related to broader, less focused titles such as 'The representation of women in film', 'Account for the popularity of *EastEnders*' or 'Voyeurism in the media'.

Problems with coursework

You probably have several coursework assignments to complete across your AS and A2 subjects, and it is worth taking the time to think about some of the problems you may encounter in managing these demanding tasks. These problems involve matters such as time management and the organisation of the materials you will be investigating and assessing for the study.

(1) At the beginning of the year the deadline seems a long way off and it is difficult to make a serious start on the work. Then suddenly the deadline is imminent and you have hardly begun.

Solution You must plan and manage your time so that you work steadily through the year rather than leaving everything to the last minute.

(2) You have notes and drafts all over the place but you cannot get started on the study itself. You are not sure what your title is or whether the work you are doing is strictly relevant.

Solution Make sure you are working to a focused question or hypothesis and spend time setting out your intention in an opening paragraph. Reread your question and alter it if it seems ambiguous or vague. Try to organise your notes systematically, too.

(3) Every time you sit down to work on your own you are interrupted or you think of something that you urgently need to do. You set aside evenings to work and then find you have achieved very little.

Solution This comes down to task avoidance. It can be difficult to concentrate and commit yourself to solid periods of work, especially early on in the study when deadlines seem far away, but you have to discipline yourself. Try working for short periods with no distractions. Break the work down into small, achievable tasks and make sure you complete them.

(4) All your subject teachers want the work in at the same time. This is probably because they have to meet similar subject deadlines for marking and moderating the work.

Solution You cannot avoid this, but if your work has been managed over the whole period allowed and you have made good progress in all subjects, this need not be a problem. Effective time management and prioritising academic work over other activities are the only answers.

Planning the Independent Study

It is worth thinking carefully before committing yourself to a topic for the study. Ask yourself honest questions.
- Are you really interested in the topic?
- Can you easily gain access to the information and materials that you need?
- Could it be made to fit in with work you are doing in other subjects?
- Is it manageable, or is it too ambitious?

Talk all these matters through with your teacher, parents and friends and, if possible, do a brief feasibility study on your topic before making a final decision. It is also important to read through the whole of this guide before you make any firm decisions.

Sample passages and comments

The sample passages below are taken from candidates' work and have been chosen to illustrate the type of material seen by examiners. They are followed by comments from an examiner's point of view.

Marking at A-level is 'positive', which means that examiners mark what they see in the way that gives most credit to candidates. They do not have 'ideal' or perfect answers in mind, and the passages are not intended to be definitive or model submissions. Instead, the aim is to show how each candidate's work matches up to specific grade criteria. Marks are awarded on a 'best fit' principle against band descriptors, and the examiner has to make a judgement as to which description best suits the work. All work should reflect the individuality of each candidate. However, writing style is important in conveying a sense of authority in your field.

> Pluralism argues that the Media has a great influence over dictating the Value Consensus in our societies through their News Consensus, which is largely defined by those who have power, otherwise known as the gatekeepers (editors, publishers i.e. Murdock). These Rules and Norms are generally agreed upon amongst of their audience. Norms and Values are very much controlled by the agenda, in which news is brought to them.

ℯ Errors of grammar, spelling and punctuation, and what the actual examiner referred to as 'poor expression', make this passage difficult to follow. Although the candidate attempts to address theories of news values and consensus, the points are hard to grasp and no clear understanding is conveyed. It is important to ensure that names of key figures like Murdoch are spelled correctly. Remember that although the emphasis is always on the positive, you ought to revise your work carefully to ensure clarity of expression. Try reading it out to a friend and asking him/her to feed back to you the point you are making. If he/she gets it wrong or doesn't understand, you probably need to clarify your phrasing.

Now compare the above with this passage:

The extremely radical question of whether Afghanistan has been rid of one oppressive regime for another lingers in many readers' minds. The Alliance soldiers are in this instance represented as figures of evil and violence, and I find myself as the reader being compelled to sympathise with the Taliban soldier who had to endure their 'vengeful' wrath. From the selection of this appalling image (a photograph of a degraded, blood-soaked Taliban soldier being abused by his captors) it can be said that the *Mirror* is not fully behind the allied action in Afghanistan and ready to debate the West's connection with the Northern Alliance. Perhaps the *Mirror* is reflecting our thoughts — as a western society we can see such acts as inhumane. However, the editor can be accused of being biased against the war and it is his ideas and assumptions that are resonant in the newspaper.

ℯ This is a very different topic but one that also concerns news values, newspaper editors and the readership. Here there is a strong sense of the writer's voice and of critical autonomy as the issues are weighed and evaluated. Qualifying phrases such as 'it can be said that' and words like 'perhaps' and 'however' help to create the measured, objective tone in this paragraph and justify the examiner's overall comment on the study: 'Excellent analysis of news production clearly placed within a wider cultural framework.'

Marking and grading

The marking process

A total of 60 marks are available for Module 5. When your work is submitted, it is marked by your teacher. If there are several Media Studies teachers in your school or college, they check between them that they are marking to the same standard. The marks are then submitted to AQA and your centre's moderator. Moderators receive work from a number of centres and have the job of ensuring that all marks are awarded fairly and that all centres are marking to the same standard.

You need to demonstrate knowledge and application of the Key Concepts, and an appreciation of relevant wider historical, social, political and economic contexts. Most importantly, you need to draw these elements together by making connections between them and your own study. Applying critical ideas and principles to your study demonstrates critical autonomy and media literacy. This aspect of the study is called the synoptic element and it is worth 25% of the Module 5 marks or 15/60. The largest element, 75% of the Module 5 marks or 45/60, is awarded for your ability to use appropriate investigative and research techniques in carrying out your study. Mark schemes provide band descriptors for a total mark, which includes both the synoptic element and the research element, and it is these band descriptors, applied on a 'best fit' basis, which decide the final mark awarded.

The AQA mark scheme

A range of characteristics describes each of the six bands in the mark scheme, and examiners have to choose the band that most closely describes the work being assessed. The mark ranges in the various bands are 51–60, 41–50, 31–40, 21–30, 11–20 and 1–10. The top-band descriptors are as follows:

51–60 marks (grade A)
- Excellent evidence of synoptic ability in drawing together concepts and ideas from different parts of the specification.
- Excellent analysis into the chosen text and related issues.
- Excellent knowledge and application of all the Key Concepts.
- Sharp focus on the key areas raised by the text chosen and related issues.
- Excellent research with excellent use of a wide range of primary and secondary sources.
- Excellent evaluation of texts chosen and related issues using the Key Concepts.
- Excellent ability to relate texts chosen to related issues and to wider historical, social, political and economic contexts.
- Writing will be fluent and controlled and the Study will be well organised and presented.
- Clear and accurate identification and referencing of sources used.
- Clearly focused hypothesis addressed and answered.

The key positive words here are *excellent, sharp, fluent* and *clear*.

The band descriptors for the 31–40 range, which is broadly in line with a grade C at A2, are as follows:
- Good evidence of synoptic ability in drawing together concepts and ideas from different parts of the specification.
- Good analysis into the chosen text and related issues.
- Good knowledge and application of all the relevant Key Concepts.
- Sound focus on the key areas raised by the chosen text and related issues.
- Sound ability to relate text chosen and related issues to wider historical, social, political and economic contexts.

- Writing will be clear, and the Study competently organised and presented.
- Most sources will be identified and referenced.
- Hypothesis is formulated and addressed.

The descriptors here are *good*, *sound*, *clear* and *competent*. The lowest band descriptors (0–10 marks) include words such as *little*, *limited* and *basic*.

Checklist for submission

Your final submission should:

- consist of a 3,000-word extended essay together with a full bibliography of all source material. There is no penalty for exceeding the word length but you should try to keep within a few hundred words of the word count. Extra material or appendices can be submitted to your teacher but will not be marked. This is merely seen as evidence of the work that you have done.
- answer a question posed in the title, investigate a topic, or test a hypothesis (a theoretical statement)
- have a clear conclusion or outcome
- be largely based on the analysis of a contemporary text or texts
- show evidence of 'critical autonomy' (your own informed opinion and judgement)
- show evidence of a lively engagement with Media Studies concepts and perspectives

Content
Guidance

This section outlines the AQA specification and explains how Module 5 fits in with the other five modules. It shows how the Independent Study complements and develops the other modules in the specification by building on areas of study, particularly those covered in Module 4. Because the range of topics for Independent Studies is so wide, it is not possible to provide a comprehensive review of the content of all the potential topics you might choose, so what follows is a selection using some of the most popular areas as examples.

Progression from AS to A2

The AQA specification explains the difference between AS and A2 modules in terms of emphasis. While in the AS modules the emphasis is on how texts work, at A2 the focus is on why texts are the way they are and the historical, social, political and economic forces that have shaped them.

According to the specification:

> The mass media arguably constitute the primary symbolic forms of contemporary western cultures. They are the most important means by which information, ideas, aesthetic experiences and entertainment are transmitted to citizens and consumers. They are also vital forces for social and cultural cohesion or exclusion and central to contemporary discussion of politics, aesthetics, social identity and cultural rights.

Candidates for the A2 examination need to demonstrate some understanding and knowledge of the ways in which the media work in our society and express this by exercising a degree of critical autonomy in the analysis of specific media texts. The content of the Independent Study should be sufficiently researched and demanding to allow candidates the opportunity to explore relevant media perspectives in some detail.

Content of the Independent Study

Terminology

The definition of the Independent Study given in the specification could not be clearer, and yet examiners report a surprising number of candidates who do not follow the principles outlined above and who consequently fail to fulfil their potential in this module. Before going any further it is therefore important to examine some of the advice provided and explain some of the terminology used.

The AQA specification describes Module 5 in the following way: 'Candidates will use the Key Concepts to investigate or research an independent area of study, which will deal with a **contemporary** text, topic or issue and its relevant **contexts**. This module will contribute to the specification's **synoptic** assessment.'

'Contemporary'

'Contemporary' is defined by the AQA specification as:

> ...being produced or released within the previous 2 years (so, for example, repeats of programmes made outside the period should not be used as central texts). However, historical texts may be used for the purpose of comparison in order to illuminate the nature of the contemporary text, but they must remain subordinate to it. Any text studied should be **appropriately conceptualised**.

'Appropriately conceptualised'

This means that texts should be considered in terms of their particular genre, medium and the period in which they are produced rather than just for themselves. For example, realism in film is a concept and treatment which has changed over time. Realism in the 1950s is not the same as realism in the twenty-first century. What felt 'real' to a 1950s audience may not seem 'real' to a contemporary audience.

'Synoptic'

Synoptic means that the study should show a wide understanding of media concepts covered in other parts of the specification. The study must concentrate on recent material and should also seek to place the material firmly in various contexts.

'Contexts'

Appropriate contexts might include 'any relevant historical, social, political or economic contexts. The contexts of production, distribution and reception might also be included. A simple text analysis of a film or a soap opera would not be appropriate' (AQA specification). Examples of relevant contexts could be the press coverage of Islam after 11 September 2001 or the representation of women in advertising in a 'post-feminist' world.

Quality of writing

Quality of written communication is assessed in all modules involving extended writing. The AQA specification states that candidates will be assessed according to their ability to:

- select and use styles and forms of writing appropriate to purpose
- organise relevant information coherently and clearly, using specialist vocabulary where appropriate
- ensure that spelling, grammar and punctuation are accurate so that meaning is clear

This is of particular relevance to Module 5, where you are writing a continuous piece of prose which expounds and develops an argument.

Further reading

Before embarking on the study, it is important to broaden your understanding of a whole range of media issues. You may find *Media Magazine*, published by the English and Media Centre, helpful in this respect. *Sight and Sound* magazine is an invaluable source of film-related articles and reviews and back copies may be available in your library. Media-related articles appear in dedicated sections of quality newspapers and the *Media Guardian*, which appears on Mondays, is particularly useful for keeping up to date with media issues. The broader your understanding of the contexts in which media products are created, the easier it will be for you to frame your study within these contexts and so achieve the expected level of debate.

Checklist for a successful study

Follow the simple rules listed below and you should be on the way to success:
- Choose your title with care and keep it focused.
- Make your chosen text the heart of your study.
- Ensure that your text has been produced or released within the 2 years previous to the commencement of your course.
- Concentrate on evaluation and analysis, not description and narrative.
- Use relevant historical texts as the basis for comparison.
- Relate your study to the Key Concepts and the wider historical, social, political or economic contexts.
- Relate your study to wider media debates and theories as appropriate.
- Make good use of work done in other modules, particularly Module 4.
- Keep to the specified number of words.
- Check your spelling, vocabulary, grammar and punctuation throughout.

Approaching the Independent Study

By the time you come to consider the Independent Study you will probably have been successful in some or all of the AS modules. The Media Studies specification is designed so that all aspects of the course are interrelated and overlapping, so by the time you are ready to undertake your Independent Study you will already have learned a great deal about the Key Concepts, media language, media content and critical approaches and will probably have found some aspects of the course particularly interesting. This could be of help to you in choosing the topic for your study, as you may wish to develop a particular interest further.

The study could develop work that you have begun in Module 4 because 25% of the marks are synoptic, which means that you are expected to draw on other aspects of the course and other modules in your study. For example, theories concerning representation covered in Module 4 could also be relevant to Module 5 work.

Links to Module 4

Your school or college will probably have chosen two options from the Module 4 specification range of four. These are:

- the production and manufacture of news
- representations
- genre
- media audiences

Think of ways in which you can make use of the materials and perspectives adopted in Module 4 to formulate your study. Examples involving the representation of women and 'male gaze' theory are developed on pp. 19–20. For the production of news topic, any study related to the selection of subject matter and the representation of social groups, issues or places will clearly draw on the 'agenda setting' and 'news values' elements covered in Module 4. Similarly, topics which focus on 'media effects' in relation to the representation of sex and violence in film, for example, or negative stereotyping of social groups, draw on audience theory together with representational issues.

As with all elements of the specification, there is considerable overlap between the Module 4 options and the study areas recommended for Module 5. This is intentional and to be encouraged as it contributes to the overall integration and coherence of your studies. While you may cover particular areas of theory as part of your Module 4 classwork, you may need to research additional related areas yourself. A list of possible sources is provided on p. 33.

Critical autonomy

Media Studies places great emphasis on students achieving 'critical autonomy'. Having studied different media perspectives and issues and become familiar with media terminology, you are encouraged to apply your knowledge and develop your own point of view. This is an important principle in preparing for the Independent Study.

Time scale

Your examination centre will tell you the deadline for submission of the completed study and you should be given plenty of time to make your choice of topic and the hypothesis or question you are going to address before embarking on the research and writing. Take time to consider the following:

- What aspect of Media Studies have you found most interesting? Could you use this as the basis for your study? For example, you may be particularly interested in the representation of girls and women in women's magazines or concepts of maleness and masculinity in men's lifestyle magazines.
- Have you any specialist knowledge or perspective that might help you choose a topic? For example, you may want to explore ethnic or regional representations or you may be in a position to make cultural or ethnic comparisons in relation to media coverage.
- Do you have any personal interests which you can direct towards the study? For example, you may be interested in sport and sports reporting or different aspects of music and music journalism.

Remember, the closer you are to the topic the more involved you will feel and the easier it will be to develop an independent critical voice. Only when you have decided on a topic area that you are interested in is it time to consider the kind of investigative task to set yourself in order to meet the requirements of the specification.

Choice of topic

Formulating your hypothesis or question

It is certainly true that some topics are more suited to the Independent Study than others, but most topics can be the basis of a successful study if the hypothesis or question is framed suitably. It is important to remember that you are investigating a situation or testing a theory and the question you set yourself must be answerable in the terms of the study specification. There are several key elements involved in designing your title, as outlined below.

Limit your investigation

This is crucial. You are only asked for 3,000 words and you must ensure that you are not trying to do too much and that your topic is not too open-ended or general.

Ask a question or set out to prove or disprove a statement

Your study has to be in the form of an argument or debate. It should be an evaluative analysis of selected material, not a descriptive catalogue of research undertaken. It is assessed on the basis of quality, not quantity.

Make sure that you can answer the question or test the hypothesis objectively

A title such as 'Tabloid coverage of Posh and Becks is unfair and intrudes into their private life' is not really a question or hypothesis, just a subjective value judgement that could lead to a study in which the candidate merely offers a personal opinion. Remember that you need to place yourself in the role of an investigator, testing the evidence using media concepts and reaching objective conclusions.

For this topic a title such as 'Tabloid obsession with celebrities such as Victoria and David Beckham leads to a distortion of news values and an increasing neglect of hard news in the popular press' could establish the hypothesis and an opening paragraph could define the area of study — perhaps comparing the news values of two tabloids with those of broadsheet titles over the same period. It is important here not to gloss over a large amount of material but to provide detailed analysis of specific content. Remember that you have to show understanding of the Key Concepts and their application to your area of study.

Remember that the study is text based

The main focus of your study must be the analysis of media texts released or produced within the previous 2 years in order to test your hypothesis or answer the question that you have set yourself. You must identify and explain your choice of texts and show how your analysis of them is relevant to your purpose. All the theoretical research you do should be directed towards this textual analysis.

Give yourself time

Don't rush into a decision over your topic and don't be afraid to change your mind. Try out ideas and allow yourself space to think about them. Make sure that your final choice is the right one for you — you will be spending several months with the subject and it must be something which interests you and with which you feel comfortable.

Subject matter

The specification offers a wide choice of subject matter and you may have your own original ideas. The exact wording of the title depends on your own interests and approach. Once again, remember that work from Module 4 might help you to choose your direction. Below is a list of topics which have proved successful:

- representation of male and female sports stars in the tabloid press
- reality TV and the 'dumbing down' of television
- 'infotainment' and the decline of 'hard news'
- American media products and the globalisation of culture
- Bollywood and the representation of Asian values
- music journalism in the age of *Pop Idol*
- 'tweeny' magazines and the commercialisation of childhood
- male and female representation issues — could be contemporary advertisements, a film, a television series or drama

- film classification, censorship and moral panics
- ethnic representation stereotypes, archetypes and alternatives
- blockbuster movie culture, formulas, successes, failures
- teenagers, role models and magazines
- the royal family soap opera — recent media coverage of specific royal personages
- the media cult of celebrity
- media effects theory tested — study of recent texts
- the tabloids and Europe/the developing world

Whatever topic you choose, you must analyse specific contemporary media texts. The specification emphasises that the bulk of the study *must* be focused on the contemporary text. Historical texts should only be used if they are part of a comparative analysis. The 2004 edition of the specification gives the example of the 2001 Tim Burton film *Planet of the Apes* being compared in terms of changing historical, social, political and economic contexts to earlier films of the same title.

How to formulate a question and define the direction of a study

The key word often used in examiner and moderator reports is 'focus'. To be successful in the Independent Study you must make sure that your title is written in such a way as to allow you to develop an argument. You should also try to centre your work on a subject in which a theoretical approach (e.g. Marxism or feminism) can be explored and an issue involving debate (e.g. positive and negative representation of males/females, ethnic groups, youth; the effects of sex and violence in media images), together with a body of research, can form the framework for your textual evaluation.

Other parts of your Media Studies course may involve looking at various aspects of media theory. For example, for the representation option in Module 4 you may be looking at Laura Mulvey's work on 'male gaze' in the representation of women in film and you could use this theory as the starting point in your own investigation.

Mulvey, writing in 1975, saw the visual pleasure of film as being structured by men for the pleasure of men. Women are objects of the male gaze both within a film narrative and also for the wider pleasure of the male audience. Much has changed since 1975 and Mulvey's theory has been criticised in some quarters, but feminists have cited it in support of their call for changes in the way images of women are constructed and perceived.

If you were going to use this theory as the basis for your study, you would need to decide whether or not you agree with its conclusions and whether or not they are still valid. You could start by asking yourself a few more questions. First you could try framing the questions using Mulvey's perspective:

Are women in film still represented in sexist ways for the entertainment and pleasure of men?

Alternatively, you could ask an open question:

Is there evidence of change in the representation of women in film?

You might adopt a more challenging and assertive viewpoint:

Do contemporary representations of women in film provide evidence of increasingly dominant roles?

Or again:

Is feminine the new masculine in action movies?

Ask yourself how you would set about answering these questions and any others you think of. Where would you look for evidence? Which texts would you focus on?

The question you finally set yourself needs to give a clear indication of your focus and to specify the texts you will be studying. In this case you might take as your working title something like the following: 'Do contemporary representations of women in film as independent, self-motivated individuals in control of their destiny and the equals of men, challenge traditional "male gaze" theory? A comparison of female leads in *Lara Croft: Tomb Raider* and *The Matrix*.'

Working with titles

Once you have embarked on your investigation it is a perfectly acceptable part of the process to modify and develop your title and your textual study as you go along. Your teacher will probably conduct tutorial sessions to give you feedback on your progress and advice on how best to continue, so the phrase 'working title' means just that — a title to work with while your arguments and ideas develop but one that can be altered as the study moves forward.

Having a poorly constructed or unsuitable title is often the source of problems encountered by students during the course of the Independent Study. Below are some real titles from students' work, some of which are more suitable than others. Spend a few minutes considering these and deciding which you think would lead to a successful study. Then read the commentaries that follow. There were several punctuation errors in the original title examples which have been corrected. While this is not regarded as a 'hanging offence', it detracts from the seriousness of the work and suggests a lack of attention to detail by the candidate. Check through all your work, remembering that mistakes of any kind in your title are particularly obvious and can let you down badly.

(1) Has the tabloid papers' intrusion into celebrities' lives become more invasive rather than newsworthy and in the public interest?

(2) Two months after the twin towers fell, the tabloid press have become less united in the support of Allied action in Afghanistan.

(3) How has Gorillaz been constructed in order to appeal to its target audience?

(4) Masculinity in crisis. How are men represented in 'lads' mags'?

(5) Media publicity has built up *Kabhi Khushi Kabhi Gham* (*K3G*) to be the most successful Bollywood film.

(1) The first title in the list is not very well framed. Which celebrities? Which tabloid papers? Over what study period? When has coverage of celebrities ever been in the 'public interest'? Exactly where is this study going? It will probably be demonstrating that tabloid coverage of celebrities is 'intrusive', in which case there is a danger that the essay will become merely a defence of the right to privacy. The title needs to challenge the wider relationship between celebrities, the press and the public, and to consider the 'news values' involved in the cult of the celebrity.

Consider what improvements would be made if the wording were to be adjusted to: 'Is the diversion of tabloid newspaper attention from hard news stories to the lives of celebrities in the public interest? A comparison of celebrity coverage and hard news in the *Independent*, the *Sun* and the *Daily Mail*, January–April 2003.'

Concepts such as news values and agenda setting are now brought in, and we can move into areas of contemporary concern such as 'infotainment' and 'dumbing down'. Particular texts are also specified, representing a cross-section of media values and institutions.

(2) The second 'question' is actually an assertion and the study will presumably demonstrate its truth. Given the diverse nature of the press and the search for a distinctive editorial voice as part of each paper's identity, increasingly divergent opinions are hardly surprising. It would have been a good idea to limit the study to two or three named publications over a specific period of time. The test of the title is whether or not it gives the candidate the opportunity to engage analytically with media issues.

(3) Titles like the third one are unfortunately very common and create difficulties for candidates. The problem is the kind of study such titles produce — usually no more than content analysis which is unchallenging and uncritical. In this case the study is likely to be simply a deconstruction of the cartoon group's origins and appeal. As it is currently phrased, the question is unlikely to lead the candidate into the more analytical discourses necessary to demonstrate 'critical autonomy' and achieve higher grades.

(4) The fourth title deals with a popular topic but is worded sloppily. Why not 'men's lifestyle magazines' rather than the colloquial 'lads' mags'? Which magazines is the student going to study, and over what period? There is no clear direction here and the title is likely to produce open-ended material. There needs to be a clear point of comparison and perhaps a question to answer. If masculinity is in crisis, as the title contends, the nature of that 'crisis' — and the evidence for it — must be assessed in the opening paragraphs.

A rephrased title might be: 'Does the representation of masculinity in recent editions of *Loaded*, *FHM* and *Maxim* (January–April 2003) provide evidence for a "crisis in masculinity"?' Now there is a clear question to address: does the style of representation suggest a crisis — yes or no? This essay could then be directed towards clear conclusions drawn from specific material.

(5) Like the second, the fifth title is a statement or assertion and is unlikely to work. In this case it is likely to produce an uncritical review of *Kabhi Khushi Kabhi Gham*'s success. There is nothing here to debate or analyse and the candidate could do a great deal of research and still only achieve a modest grade. Something along these lines would be much better: 'Does the representation of Asian values, relationships and culture in *Kabhi Khushi Kabhi Gham* (*K3G*), the most successful Bollywood film to date, challenge or reinforce existing Asian stereotypes?' This would provide a focus for the study and a source of debate.

This analysis shows that it is worth reworking your title with the help of your tutor as you research and develop your study to make sure that you have a clear sense of direction. This will help you to achieve your potential in the assessment.

Research methods

The content of your Independent Study depends largely on the success of your research, so it is important to undertake research in a methodical and structured way.

It may be tempting to submit copies of important texts and visual material with your study to show the examiner how well you have researched your topic, but there is no need to do this. It is sufficient for your study to analyse these materials and for them to be listed in the bibliography. All the research you undertake for your study is valuable, even though the final submission is only 3,000 words and there will not be space to discuss everything directly. Well-researched studies always stand out from those based on thinner research. You are expected to undertake both primary and secondary research.

Primary research

The primary research is your own reading and evaluation of media texts, together with content analysis. For example, you might watch an evening's television advertisements to see how women or ethnic minorities are represented. You would need to log your viewing and record the results systematically. You might wish to select some of the material for a specific textual study. Remember to record all the details for inclusion in your bibliography.

Secondary research

Secondary research is your use of research work by other theorists and academics and any other critical or review material. You must make organised notes on your readings, identifying sources, works and authors and evaluating the material. A research log book is provided on pp. 35–36 as an example of how this can be done, but remember that this is to help you to organise your research materials and does not form part of the submission and assessment.

Bibliography

You need to compile a thorough bibliography, which includes all the textbooks, magazines, films and other materials you may have referred to in the course of your study. It is a good idea to make a note of everything you consult as you go along. The bibliography is an important part of the submitted work as appendices and other support materials are not marked, so it is worth taking the time to make sure it is comprehensive and thorough. The examiner will look through your bibliography to see how you have gathered your materials together and you need to record the various elements systematically (see 'Assembling the pieces' on pp. 36–40).

Key Concepts

The assessment criteria for this module stress the need to cover the Key Concepts of Media Studies. You are probably already very familiar with these as you will encounter them in all the units of the specification. If you find acronyms helpful, keep in mind that the initial letters of the Key Concepts spell **GRAVIL**:

Genre and narrative
Representation
Audience
Values and ideology
Institutions
Language of media

The Key Concepts underlie all media products and all the modules in the A-level specification. In pursuing your Independent Study you need to bring them to the surface as you develop your analysis. Keep them in mind when undertaking your research as they will help you to develop an all-important angle on your topic as well as providing you with headings to direct your investigation.

The assessment criteria also stress the importance at A2 of demonstrating your under-standing of the historical, social, political and economic aspects of the topic under study. You therefore need to investigate the relevant background materials and the theor-etical perspectives involved in your subject. It is useful to consider how theory and theorists relate to the Key Concepts, and the following outlines offer reminders of individuals and approaches, together with some background.

Genre and narrative theories

All media texts belong to a genre and involve a narrative of some description, and in relating your study to Module 4 work you may wish to refer to theories of genre and narrative. **Richard Dyer** is a film theorist whose work on genre has been influential. A clear outline of his approach is given in *The Media Student's Book* by **Jill Branston** and **Roy Stafford** (Routledge, 1999). The work of **Propp**, **Todorov**, **Levi-Strauss** and **Barthes** on narrative is also well known and is summarised in most media textbooks. It is often cited by candidates and should be used with care, for reference only.

A narrative account of a range of theories is not the right way to start your study. Be aware of them as you go about your research, but only refer to them if they are relevant. Don't spend time trying to force a narrative into a particular theoretical framework — it doesn't serve any useful purpose unless it is the actual focus of your title. Comments such as 'This proves Propp's theory' in the course of your essay are unlikely to be relevant or helpful.

Representation

Many Independent Studies involve aspects of representation, and the concept offers a fruitful approach to media issues as well as being a study area in Module 4. For topics concerning ethnic representation, **Stuart Hall**'s work on black and African-Caribbean representation in British media is an important starting point. **Laura Mulvey** is often referenced by students for her 'male gaze' theory in relation to the representation of women. Although Mulvey still writes regularly on film, it should be remembered that much of her critique of the use of women in cinema is now over a quarter of a century old. There are many studies of representation in academic media texts and an internet search produces good results too. You may wish to consider representations of young people and youth culture, for which **Dick Hebdidge**'s *Subculture: The Meaning of Style* (Methuen, 1997) might be a good starting point, or more recently *Popular Music and Youth Culture* by **Andy Bennett** (Palgrave Macmillan, 2000).

Audience

Audience research, another Module 4 study area, is almost certain to play a part in your Independent Study. All media make the assumption that an audience exists and is in some way affected by a media product — people may be entertained, amused, gratified, persuaded, indoctrinated, corrupted etc. An audience which is indifferent to a media product to the point of disengagement is not of much interest to a media producer.

In conducting the study, you are likely to be a part of the audience for the product yourself, and you need to establish a clear distinction between you as consumer and you as objective critic and analyst. Audience theories are framed in terms of **media effects** in most Media Studies textbooks. Questions asked often take the following basic form: 'What does the media do to the audience?' or 'What does the audience do with the media?'

The question of how people are affected by the media has concerned moralists and politicians since the emergence of the modern mass media in the late nineteenth century. In particular, film was seen as an important tool of propagandists and social engineers, from the early days of the Russian Revolution and the films of **Eisenstein** in Soviet Russia to **Leni Riefenstahl**'s *Triumph of the Will* (1934) in Nazi Germany.

Moralists from the early days of mass media saw film and printed media as dangerous and subversive of decency and mainstream orthodox values. A wide range of media products have been seen as a threat to the moral order — from late nineteenth-century 'dime novels' (known as 'penny dreadfuls' in England), early 1920s Tom Mix Westerns, 1950s American horror comics, classics such as *The Wild One* (1954), *Rebel Without a Cause* (1955), *Last Tango in Paris** (1972), to films like *Child's Play 3** (1991), *I Spit on Your Grave** (1978), and more recently *Natural Born Killers** (1994) and *Crash** (1996). In 1930s America, the Hayes Office Production Code (1930) was designed to protect the public from 'unsuitable' or 'degenerate' material, and its legacy of censorship affected the content of films until the late 1960s. The office was dissolved in 1966 by the US Supreme Court, which stated that the office's practices constituted censorship. As a result, cinema audiences in the late 1960s were exposed to images of sex and violence not seen since the early days of cinema. Arthur Penn's *Bonnie and Clyde* (1967) shocked audiences with scenes of victims' bodies penetrated by bullets, previously banned under the Hayes Code. The current activities of the UK-based Media Watch organisation, the successor to Mary Whitehouse's campaigning National Viewers' and Listeners' Association, show that there is continuing vigilance in some quarters about morally threatening material.

Propaganda was claimed to have a direct influence on the masses, as argued in the pessimistic theorising of the Marxist **Frankfurt School**. According to the Frankfurt theorists, resistance to dominant ideology was useless as it was all ultimately subverted by consumer capitalism and incorporated into mainstream mass culture. In **Marcuse**'s phrase, this created 'one-dimensional man'. **Orwell**'s seminal work

Nineteen Eighty-Four (written in the year 1948) painted a grim picture of mass manipulation by an oligarchic power elite using the cinema and the 'Telescreen' to control ideology and direct behaviour.

In the 1930s and 1940s American pollsters and politicians also sought evidence to establish how public opinion could be formed and manipulated at election time. **Walter Lippman** (1889–1974) was an influential figure throughout this period. His 1922 work *Public Opinion* (Free Press, 1997), with its early study of stereotypes, remains an important text. Media effects theory usually starts with the '**hypodermic needle**' model, which assumes that the all-powerful media manipulate a passive mass audience and change attitudes and behaviour directly with the 'injection' of a media 'drug'. Although often quoted by students, this theory is largely discredited as being too simplistic to describe how a pluralist, differentiated, media-literate contemporary audience engages with media products.

Later theories such as the **two-step flow** or **opinion leadership** models, associated with Katz and Lazarsfeld and Schramm and Gerbner respectively, begin to differentiate the mass audience and see it as being both more diverse and more actively engaged with media products. **Stuart Hall**'s contribution to the effects debate emphasises the **ideological effect** and the **Gramscian** concept of **hegemony** (ideological domination effected through the media by power elites). Sometimes called the '**drip drip theory**', this emphasises the almost subliminal power of messages repeated over time to structure and constrain the independent thought of the audience. Audiences are seen as bowing to the 'common sense' principle of consensus in support of the ideological status quo, which always serves to reinforce existing power elites. However, Hall's emphasis on the way an audience 'reads' a media product allows for considerable individualisation of response and 'resistance' to what he calls the 'preferred reading', i.e. that intended or assumed by the media producer.

Such resistance gives rise to **negotiated** and even **oppositional** stances where audience members refuse a message and draw an opposite conclusion from the one intended. In early 2003, in spite of concerted efforts at persuasion by politicians and large sections of the British media, the majority of British people remained sceptical and solidly against British involvement in the war in Iraq — a classic example of oppositional reading at work. The relationship between politicians, the public and the media has become an issue of major concern in contemporary British society, particularly in relation to the concept of '**spin**' (the ability of those in power to manipulate and control the presentation of their actions and policies to the public in order to serve their own interests). 'Spin' was made notorious by the e-mail sent by a government media adviser on the morning of 11 September 2001, which read: 'Now is a good time to bury bad news.'

Inoculation theory suggests that frequent exposure to the same media message dulls the impact of the message. For example, television and newspaper images of starving children and dead people lose their power to shock over time; likewise, sexual or violent images become more acceptable the more they are seen.

Uses and gratifications theory flatters an audience into believing it has real choice to 'pick and mix' from media products according to lifestyle, self-image and personal needs. It fails to allow for the fact that media producers operating within a cultural, ideological and economic framework determine the choice of media products available. Supporters of the theory argue that as media industries are market driven (i.e. responsive to demand pressures), audiences get what they want. Marxists argue that what audiences want is determined by the dominant capitalist ideology — a form of false consciousness. This means that people don't recognise what their real interests are and just accept the choices offered without question. Marxists argue that this doesn't represent real freedom or real choice.

Many theories of audience developed from French **semiological** and film theory emphasise the subjective primacy of the viewer or audience in the construction of meaning. The writings of **Goddard**, **Foucault**, **Baudrillard**, **Lyotard**, **Barthes** and others are significant here. This approach focuses on the importance of the unique intellectual and cultural make-up of the individual in **making sense** of media products — what the audience does with the media, not the other way round.

Contemporary approaches to audience theory also address the issue of '**dumbing down**' — the way in which difficult and complex material is simplified and turned into entertainment to appeal to wider audiences in an undemanding way. The term is often applied in 'high'-cultural contexts. For example, Baz Luhrmann's contemporary film version of *Romeo + Juliet* (1996) was criticised by some for its populist adaptation of Shakespeare's classic play. Others felt that the film brought new life to the play for a contemporary audience.

If your topic involves censorship and the arguments surrounding the exposure of audiences to sex, violence and behaviour deemed anti-social such as drug taking or crime, **Guy Cumberbatch** is an important source of research summaries. The **British Board of Film Classification** (BBFC) produces a valuable website and student pack covering the history and evolution of film classification and censorship.

All the theorists named and theories outlined above provide a backdrop to your topic and when, if appropriate, you research them more thoroughly they should help you to develop your analysis. They are only useful if you can apply them — don't make the mistake of trying to make your material fit the theory. Read widely and then develop your own well-informed voice. That's what 'critical autonomy' is all about.

Values and ideology

All media products are produced within a framework of values, even an advertisement for a new dishwasher or a Harry Potter film. Being able to identify the core values and assumptions behind a media product is an important skill and one which students often find difficult to master. Where, you might ask, are the values and ideology in something as seemingly harmless and entertaining as a Tom and Jerry cartoon? Yet these have been subjected to serious criticism by those who claim they demonstrate repeatedly that the use of maximum violence to solve disputes is always a successful and valid strategy.

Sometimes the least obvious products contain the most significant ideological messages. For example, no one would now argue that soap powder adverts from the 1950s to the 1970s, showing women competing against one another to achieve the perfect washed white shirt for their husbands, were not sexist and diminishing, representing women as being defined by their relationship to the dominant, bread-winning male and being obsessed with domestic trivia and petty rivalry. These adverts were not judged 'ideologically' in this way in their time, but have since been re-evaluated as a result of challenges levelled at dominant patriarchal values by feminist critics.

Before you embark on your study, spend a little time considering what ideological values are reflected in the material you are analysing. For example, all advertisements for designer clothes suggest an ideal person (the model and prospective buyer) whose lifestyle and appearance are validated by the attention of the camera (conferring celebrity) and the clothes being worn (status badge and logo). Such adverts imply that observers who identify with the image can achieve it by spending money on the product and attempting to mirror the appearance of the model. According to this view, having and spending money is the key to all activities, relationships, values, status and human happiness.

You may need to consider the cultural origins of the media product you are analysing to assess whether or not it carries the value system of a particular culture or ideology. For example, American cultural products dominate the globe, with over 70% of the world market share being of US or US corporate origin. Does this constitute **'cultural imperialism'**? Does it mean that all issues and value systems in the world are reinterpreted and presented through American eyes? American versions of the folk stories of other cultures, such as Disney's *Aladdin* (1992), remodel the stories in ways which please western audiences and reflect western values. Periods of history such as the bombing of Pearl Harbor and the Normandy landings of the Second World War are rewritten in such a way as to emphasise American heroism and diminish the roles played by other nations in the real-life events (e.g. *Pearl Harbor* (2001), *Saving Private Ryan* (1998)). Non-American nationalities are often stereotyped or caricatured in ways that encourage negative views of their national identity and the roles they played. Reinterpretation of this kind is not only applied to non-western cultures. Even a European product such as the Spanish film *Open Your Eyes* (1997) has been remade as *Vanilla Sky* (2001), losing its Spanish cultural setting and treatment and being reworked as an American 'mainstream' product and a vehicle for its star, Tom Cruise. What implications does this tendency have for maintaining the variety of worldwide cultural products and the fair representation of different cultural values?

Try to look objectively at your subject matter, get under the surface meanings to the essential value system, and find out what lies beneath.

Institutions

Where does a media product come from? Who makes it available and why? Whose interests does it serve? Why is it made the way it is? How much does it cost? Who gains from its production? These questions focus on an awareness of the industrial context in which media are produced. The worldwide range and power of media industries from AOL Time-Warner to News Corporation (often associated with global-isation) are well documented and students often cite Rupert Murdoch as the 'Darth Vader' of the 'Evil Empire', bent on world domination.

Not all media institutions can be caricatured as predatory, insatiable monsters devouring world culture, but matters relating to globalisation and the global reach of many multinationals are often relevant. For example, in early 2003 an article in the *Media* supplement in the *Guardian* demonstrated by a comparative analysis how all of Murdoch's newspapers in Britain, the USA, Australia and New Zealand were taking exactly the same line on the possibility of war with Iraq. This was not a coincidence, according to the article, but reflected Murdoch's interfering control over his editors. The newspaper proprietor Richard Desmond uses the *Daily Express*, the *Sunday Express* and the *Star* to advertise his *OK* magazine and other business interests — even articles and scoops are shared. The USA dominates the world's film industry and awards itself the top prizes at ceremonies designed to further reinforce its dominance. Low-budget, 'alternative' and European films have difficulty in attracting distributors in Britain and remain largely unknown and unseen by British audiences. In addition, according to its critics, including Murdoch's Sky TV, the BBC uses its guaranteed income from the licence fee to compete unfairly with commercial channels.

Ask yourself what institutions lie behind the products you are examining and how they help to shape them. *Ben's Media Guide* and the *Guardian Media Guide* contain valuable information on ownership, regulation, market positioning, readership and finance.

Language of media

The language used by the media to address an audience will have formed part of your work in Module 1, and the deconstruction of the media products you are analysing will form part of your Independent Study. By the time you come to write it, you should feel sufficiently comfortable with the vocabulary and concepts of semiology to use them as appropriate.

Terms such as **denotation** (the literal, obvious meaning of something) and **connotation** (the sociocultural and 'personal' associations of a sign) can be applied easily to all media products and the language of signs is equally flexible. **Signification** (the meaning of signs) is the key to all media meanings, and exploring the way media language creates meaning through rules of combination (**syntagm**) and choice (**paradigm**) is the easiest way to deconstruct any media product. **Anchoring** captions, slogans or titles define and focus most images. Describing **iconography** and the use of specific *mise-en-scène* — **montage**, **lighting** and **camera** and **editing** techniques — when discussing film also demonstrate understanding of media language.

Remember that these terms are tools to be used to explore how meanings are created, not a burdensome jargon, half understood and applied self-consciously like words from a foreign language. If you are not comfortable with certain terms, don't use them. Find your own voice and explore media meaning in words that have meaning for you. Remember that there are no right or wrong answers in this kind of assignment.

Wider contexts

At A2 you are expected to be more aware of the circumstances in which media products have been created. For example, although it is not about war, the Martin Scorsese classic *Taxi Driver** (1976) involves a lead character who can be seen as a victim of the Vietnam War. The Stanley Kubrick 'sword and sandals' classic *Spartacus* (1960), produced at the height of the east–west Cold War when Hollywood was producing anti-Soviet propaganda, opens with a narrative voice-over describing the struggle of enslaved peoples against a dictator. During the same period similar epics such as *Ben Hur* (1959), *Quo Vadis* (1951) and *The Robe* (1953) emphasise the struggle of early Christianity against the power of pagan Rome, mirroring the 'Christian' ideology of America in its struggle with the atheist Soviet Union. Similarly, early 1950s sci-fi movies based on narratives of alien invasion and take-over reflect the period's Cold War paranoia and the fear of communist infiltration of the USA.

Background knowledge of factors such as these furthers your understanding of a text and may help explain how it came to be constructed the way it is. In other words, the context in which a media artefact is produced reflects the politics, values and ideologies of its time. Your research is bound to involve you in placing your topic in a social, economic and historical framework. For example, if you were researching the representation of women in women's magazines you would concentrate on contemporary texts but would probably make a historical comparison too — perhaps with women's magazines in the 1950s, 1960s and 1970s. You would need to take account of stereotypes of women in those decades, shifts in representation and so on. Social, economic and political contexts would involve changes in women's roles in the home and at work, alterations in their relations with men, their greater economic independence, and the growth of feminism as a political force.

The contextualising of media products is an area candidates often have difficulty with because of their own uncertainty as to the sequence of cultural, political, social and economic change during the course of the twentieth century. Dates, events and movements often seem to run together, overlap or lose their order in candidates' attempts to summarise half a century of change in one paragraph. To avoid falling into this trap, ensure that all your observations are grounded in specific knowledge.

Example: the role and status of women

Candidates often make assertions about women's liberation and changes in the representation of women, without any real understanding of the course of these changes. Comparisons of a 'then and now' nature ('women used to stay at home and do housework but now they are more equal') are simplistic generalisations which are rarely of any value in media analysis. For example, many candidates discussing representations of women do not appear to be aware of the role of women in munitions factories and in driving ambulances and buses while men were away in combat during the First World War. This transformation of women's roles and the breakdown of traditional 'tied' relationships (e.g. the domestic servant) was reflected both in the achievement of the first stage of female suffrage in 1918 and in the subsequent 1920s 'liberation' of women in fashion terms. The representation of the powerful controlling matriarchal female robot 'Marie' in Fritz Lang's *Metropolis* (1927) pre-dates Angelina Jolie's 'flesh and blood' interpretation of a computer game character in *Lara Croft: Tomb Raider* by over 70 years. Similarly, the 1920s 'vamp' is an obvious precursor of the film noir *femme fatale*; and Mae West made a bid for the sexual liberation of women in the 1930s. In the same period Marlene Dietrich's portrayal of Catherine the Great of Russia in *The Scarlet Empress* (1934) showed a powerful, manipulative, controlling woman as a sexual predator. All of these examples illustrate non-submissive roles and representations of women long before the birth of the 'women's lib' movement.

The total involvement of women in industry and the armed services during the Second World War is also glossed over or ignored by many candidates when discussing female roles in films. Feisty, independent, unconventional female characters, such as those played by Katherine Hepburn in the 1930s and 1940s and Vivien Leigh's Scarlett O'Hara in *Gone with the Wind* (1939), are usually overlooked when claims are made about the originality of contemporary representations of powerful women in titles such as *Erin Brokovich* (2000).

Many issues concerning the role of women relate to their lack of economic power and the legal status of marriage and divorce, factors which made it difficult for women to survive on their own in low-paid work and made independence difficult to achieve. However, the model of the heroic woman striking out on her own regardless of convention or economic hardship dates back at least to Ibsen's play *A Doll's House* which scandalised London audiences in the 1880s and 1890s as the heroine walked out on her chauvinist husband, slamming the door at the end of the final act. Saving a marriage and tolerating a dull but loving husband through the sacrifice of personal happiness and desire was the eventual choice of another strong, heroic female played by Celia Johnson in *Brief Encounter* (1946). The film perhaps suggested that after a long period of disruption and trauma caused by the Second World War, frustrated and bored housewives should accept their lot and return to traditional family values in the interests of family unity and 'duty'. The use of flashback with voice-over narrative by Celia Johnson reflected the secret and unvoiced emotions, frustrations and loneliness of many women of the time. This same theme of a return to traditional roles after wartime upheaval was also present in American movies of the period, although the predominance of film noir representations of the *femme fatale* sends a very different message. Interestingly, a classic female lead of the period, Lauren Bacall, in a 2002 interview lamented the lack of strong female roles in contemporary cinema.

You are not expected to have an advanced understanding of the social, political and economic history of the twentieth century, but you must read thoroughly around your chosen topic and place it in a basic chronological and cultural framework. Avoid making sweeping generalisations about complex subjects by doing careful and relevant research. Your tutor is there to give you guidance on the direction and depth of your study. Remember, too, that the major concern of your work must be the contemporary text.

Finding the information

Starting out

Before you start your research it is a good idea to make an outline plan of the various sources you think will be useful and where you will find them. You also need to find out how recent they are by looking at publication dates and the examples and case studies they use. For example, the subject of women and cinema is covered thoroughly in the fields of sociology, film, media and cultural studies. However, some of the studies in these areas may be 20 years old and you must take this into consideration when applying their arguments to contemporary texts. This could help you with the 'historical' understanding expected in your work at A2.

You are also expected to introduce media perspectives and theory when analysing your key text(s). This doesn't mean just inserting theoretical extracts and definitions, but looking at your text(s) and topic from a theoretical point of view. Try incorporating a theoretical perspective into your title, e.g. 'To what extent are traditional theories of "male gaze", as developed by Laura Mulvey, still relevant to the representation of women in film?' This is a good way of ensuring that you engage with theoretical issues from the outset of your study.

Once again, using the representation of women and the concept of 'male gaze' as an example, a good starting point might be to find out what Laura Mulvey actually said. Her essay was entitled 'Visual pleasures and narrative cinema' and this is easily found with an internet search using the author's name and the essay title. It would be worth looking up feminist film theory, and *Feminist Film Theory: A Reader* (ed. S. Thornham, Edinburgh University Press, 1999) would be a good starting point, with plenty of further leads in the bibliography. You should also look at back issues of magazines like *The Media Magazine* and *Sight and Sound* (many libraries keep back copies for at least 2 years). *Women and Film: A Sight and Sound Reader* (eds P. Cook, and P. Dodd, Scarlet Press, 1993) is a useful collection of film analysis and reviews.

The Independent Study must be all your own work and all source material must be referenced. Don't be tempted to plagiarise — examiners can always tell when work is not your own.

Suggested sources

The following list is not intended to be comprehensive, but it provides you with some pointers. Many texts will have further relevant works listed in their bibliographies and it is worth looking through these. The topics chosen are based on the most popular areas of study.

Youth culture and popular music

Bennett, A. (2000) *Popular Music and Youth Culture: Youth, Identity and Place*, Palgrave Macmillan.
Frith, S. (1998) *Performing Rites*, Oxford Paperbacks.
Gelder, K. and Thornton, S. (eds) (1997) *The Subcultures Reader*, Routledge.
Hebdige, D. (1989) *Subculture: The Meaning of Style*, Routledge.
McRobbie, A. (1999) *In the Culture Society: Art, Fashion and Popular Music*, Routledge.
McRobbie, A. (2000) *Feminism and Youth Culture*, Macmillan.
Thompson, K. (1997) *Moral Panics*, Routledge.

Representation of women

Gauntlett, D. (2002) *Media, Gender and Identity: An Introduction*, Routledge.
Hargreaves, J. (1994) *Sporting Females*, Routledge.
Hollows, J. Hutchins, W. M. and Jancovitch, M. (eds) (2000) *The Film Studies Reader*, Arnold Press.
Mulvey, L. (1989) *Visual and Other Pleasures*, Macmillan.
Thornham, S. (ed.) (1999) *Feminist Film Theory: A Reader*, Edinburgh University Press.
Turner, G. (1993) *Film as Social Practice*, Routledge.

Media effects debates

Barker, M. (ed.) (1984) *The Video Nasties: Freedom and Censorship in the Media*, Pluto Press.
Barker, M. and Petley, J. (1997) *Ill Effects: The Media/Violence Debate (Communication and Society)*, Taylor and Francis.
Bovill, M. and Livingstone, S. (1999) *Young People*, New Media.
Cohen, S. (2002, 30th anniversary edn) *Folk Devils and Moral Panics*, Routledge.
Docherty, D. (1990) *Violence in Television Fiction*, John Libby.
French, K. (1995) *Screen Violence*, Routledge.

Resources

Textbooks and libraries

Textbooks, libraries and resource centres are the obvious first port of call, although most course textbooks will not cover your topic in sufficient detail to be useful on their own. Libraries are full of underused specialist texts. Make proper use of libraries and resource centres and don't be shy about asking for assistance.

Although some school and college libraries will not stock the particular text that you want, if you know the title, author and publisher, or the ISBN, they will be able to order it for you through the inter-library loan system. Magazines, newspapers and BFI publications are also available on the internet.

Examiners often comment on how little use students make of established academic texts and theories in any particular field of study. With lengthy academic texts, don't try to read every word. Read the introduction, skim through individual chapters to get the feel of the work, read the conclusions of chapters to see what points are being made, and end by reading the overall conclusion.

Back copies of newspapers and periodicals are invaluable, and resource centre staff will often help you locate materials far more quickly than you can find them on your own. **Ben's Media Guide** and the **Guardian Media Guide** are useful reference works for all aspects of media institution ownership, audience and regulation.

The internet

Where internet research is concerned, there is likely to be too much information at your disposal, rather than too little. The problem is quality and relevance. Much of the material on the internet is of doubtful quality and you should be highly selective when downloading it. Your main task is to sift through it and decide what is really of use to you. Think carefully about your search criteria and try to be as precise as possible (e.g. by using names of particular authors rather than entering broad subject areas). Beware of media studies sites which offer instant answers and whole essays — copying work is a serious offence, and there is no guarantee that the information will be relevant or accurate.

Most newspapers and magazines have websites with back issues of their publications. The **Audit Bureau of Circulations** and the **BBFC** have valuable sites, at **www.auditbureau.org.au** and **www.bbfc.co.uk** respectively.

e-mail

Companies and publishers are overwhelmed with requests and unsolicited e-mails. e-mail is not an effective method of conducting research, and, even if you do get some responses, you should not rely on it wholly.

Advertising agencies

Agencies can sometimes be persuaded to send you useful campaign information with plenty of glossy sample materials, but they are often difficult to contact directly. Many websites exist for individual agencies, and company names and addresses can be found in *Ben's Media Directory*, available in central libraries.

The text

Don't forget that the text is the most important aspect and source of your study and that all your background research should be used to explore and illuminate your textual analysis. Your research essay should not be 'bolted on' to a text review — the work must be integrated. Remember not to give a narrative or descriptive account of the text in question. You should be referencing selected elements to illustrate and explain the arguments you are making, never just telling the story or providing character sketches.

Audience surveys and questionnaires

As this is an academic, text-based study, questionnaires, focus groups and audience attitude surveys are not appropriate research methods and should not be used.

Recording your progress

Combing through academic textbooks, magazines and other materials can be tedious. How do you know you are getting anywhere? How can you evaluate what you are achieving? You cannot afford the time to do a full content analysis of all the texts you consult.

A research log book could help you to keep tabs on your work. Look at the following example. The topic is: 'Is female representation in contemporary action movies still subject to the "male gaze"?'

Research log book

Source: book
Title: 'Visual pleasures and narrative cinema' (essay)
Author: Laura Mulvey
Publication date: 1975
Topic: Male gaze theory and how women are made subjects of male gaze in cinema.

GRAVIL check: Genres, representation and audience values and ideology all covered well. Institution could be mainstream cinema, language is the construction of the shot and *mise-en-scène*.

Synopsis: Cinema images constructed by men for men. Women are objects of male pleasure and cameras linger on the female body for benefit of male gaze.

Relevance to study: Essential. Mulvey is a key theorist and quoted by everybody. Essay will try to establish whether her theory is still relevant by deconstructing contemporary texts. It is dated (1975) — key question is whether it still applies. Anything more recent by her or others?

Quotations: *[There will be plenty — jot them down as you go.]*

Conclusions: Really useful — a core text. Need to check references to Mulvey in other works to see what other people think/say about her — check indexes. Check her other more recent publications for relevance.

This is an example of a possible logbook layout, but you may prefer to design your own. Whatever you decide, remember that it needs to make sense to you and must be easy to refer to and follow. What you must try to ensure is a sense of personal progress and achievement — a feeling that none of the time you are spending on the study is being wasted. However you organise your notes, remember to keep a detailed record of all your sources to include in your bibliography.

The Independent Study gives you an opportunity to develop skills of research and analysis that will be important at university, where you will be expected to do most of your work on your own. Research means much more than just browsing the shelves of the learning resource centre hoping that you find a relevant text. Decide what you are looking for, read it analytically once you have found it, and always try to make the best use of your time. The limit of 3,000 words means that quality and not quantity is required and the quality of your research will directly affect the quality of the final product.

Assembling the pieces

The length of the study is 3,000 words with an allowance of 10% either way. However, you are unlikely to do justice to the topic in fewer than 3,000 words and are likely to lose focus if you go much above 3,300. If you are conscientious and have spent an appropriate amount of time on research and preparation, you will probably have too much material and too many words and will need to do some judicious selecting and cutting. If you are struggling to reach 3,000 words, you might need to do more work on the basics.

Possible problems

Problem 1

You have assembled a vast amount of media sociological research — say on the effects of audience exposure to violence in the media. You have details of studies and experiments, including the Jamie Bulger case and *Child's Play 3** (1991), details of the Bandura 'Bobo doll' experiment from your psychology course, evidence on the damaging effects on children of exposure to media violence from **www.mediawatchuk.org** (a pro-censorship watchdog body), a psychology magazine article which says it has no effect at all, and a 20-page explanation of current video and film classification policy from the BBFC. You also have a copy of the Video Recordings Act. Using this material, you have already written a 3,000-word theoretical essay on violence in the media without having started work on your texts.

> **Solution**
> Your task now is to cut, summarise and direct your material to your textual study, which must be the focus of the submission. Unless you can contextualise your research and direct it towards the text, it will seem unrelated and lacking in focus. Some of it may be out-dated and irrelevant, for example the Jamie Bulger and 'Bobo' material; some may deserve just a passing reference. Concentrate on contemporary subject matter and relate the research to it. Don't be afraid to cut out unnecessary material — it could improve your mark. If you find this difficult, ask a friend to read it through for you and suggest cuts. Your tutor will also give you advice on what direction to take.

Problem 2

You cannot find enough relevant research material, and what you have doesn't seem to help. You have done a lengthy textual deconstruction, but it reads like a content analysis. The study ends with a feeling of 'so what?' rather than a conclusion.

> **Solution**
> It sounds as though you have lost direction. Go back to your title. What did you set out to achieve? Does the title still relate to the work you have done? Can you rephrase the title to make your deconstruction work more relevant? What are your conclusions? These are probably more important than much of your content analysis — remember, you are expected to answer a question or demonstrate the truth or falsity of a hypothesis. Be prepared to change direction and seek guidance from your teacher to help concentrate your efforts in the time remaining.

Problem 3

You set out to demonstrate that there have been no changes in ethnic stereotyping in recent British television productions like *Babyfather*, but find to your surprise that there have. All your research is based on Stuart Hall's 1970s critique of the representation of African-Caribbeans on British television.

Solution

Use your findings to challenge the continuing validity of Hall's original research and try to find more recent research material as a comparison. Adapt your title and let what you find lead your conclusion. Remember that the assessment criteria require you to develop your critical autonomy and this is a good way to show it. Remember too that there is no right or wrong answer.

Format

The usual way to present the Independent Study is as a continuous piece of prose divided into paragraphs, which develops the argument progressively from introduction to conclusion. It may be annotated with footnotes, if appropriate, and should be followed by a comprehensive bibliography listing all your sources by category.

You do not need to provide headings for specific 'research' or 'analysis' sections, although there is no penalty should you wish to do so. However, there seems little advantage in adopting this approach and the best work is often presented as closely argued, progressive paragraphs.

Your **introduction** should provide a brief outline of the context and purpose of the study and can serve as a 'synoptic' element. It should set out your intentions and provide direction for the rest of the work and you should take the time to ensure that it is effective.

The **main body** of the work should have a clear structure, with paragraphs developing your ideas, arguments and textual analysis. Remember to signal a change of topic or direction by starting a new paragraph. The structure of your work will help you to develop your points effectively.

Your **conclusion** is vital. Candidates often finish a study without a conclusion, throwing away the opportunity to tie up loose ends and make a perceptive or definitive comment on the outcome of the work undertaken. The conclusion needs time and effort and should emerge from the arguments presented.

Footnotes

It is a good idea to use footnotes. When you mention a theorist or a source of information, insert an asterisk and put a note at the bottom of the page giving details of the relevant publication or source. This is regarded as good practice by examiners and gives clear evidence of your research in the body of the essay.

Bibliography

The bibliography is an essential part of your submission. AQA does not expect candidates to provide copies of magazine or newspaper articles, photographs, videos, questionnaires or any other research materials. Everything that you have researched must be listed in your bibliography, which for this reason should be as detailed as possible. If you have made detailed and organised notes as you conduct your research, you should have all the information you need to compile the bibliography.

Categorise your sources under appropriate headings like the examples below:
- **primary texts** (i.e. those chosen for your study)
- **secondary materials**, including:
  - textbooks
  - academic texts
  - journals and periodicals
  - newspapers
  - magazines
  - the internet
  - television/radio broadcasts

You must include full details of your primary texts. For films state the director, date, stars and production/distribution company. Take the time to write out your secondary sources in detail, too, not forgetting names of publishers and authors for textbooks; dates for newspaper articles, magazines and television/radio broadcasts; web addresses for internet sites. All this information helps an examiner to assess the volume and range of your research and award marks accordingly.

Try to consult a range of sources and do not rely on only one — for example, a listing of internet sites alone would not be considered an adequate bibliography. Aim to consult the core academic texts in the field you are studying and, if in doubt, ask your teacher for advice.

Appendices

You do not need to include appendices and any you submit will not be marked, although an examiner or moderator may glance through them. Do not submit videos, audio tapes, questionnaires or other collated research materials. You may wish to include relevant magazine images used in analysis, but this is not strictly necessary as the content should be made clear in the body of your study and an appropriate footnote will serve the purpose of identifying the piece. The majority of Independent Studies are submitted with no additional materials and this is the acceptable norm.

Revision

Make sure that you give yourself plenty of time for a final revision of your work, incorporating last-minute corrections and changes that can make all the difference. However, remember that your teacher is expected to mark and annotate your submitted work, so beware of substituting your 'final' copy with another pristine last minute print-off — your teacher may have already marked the earlier version. Look out for errors in spelling, grammar and punctuation — they do not actually lead to the deduction of marks, but if they obscure your meaning (e.g. through ambiguous phrasing) then your final assessment may be affected.

Administration

Remember that you have to fill in the details on the AQA candidate mark sheet yourself and sign and date the sheet. Check that your final study title is the one entered on your mark sheet as mistakes sometimes occur. The completed study should be clearly identified with your name, candidate number and centre number, and should be submitted in an appropriate document wallet. Inserting individual sheets of paper into plastic wallets causes unnecessary complications during the marking and moderation process and should be avoided.

Assessment
&
Examples

This section is designed to show you what examiners will be looking for in your Independent Study. As it is not possible to include studies of 3,000 words, extracts from seven different Independent Studies are reproduced. Each example is interspersed with examiner comments (indicated by the icon *e*). Some of the samples are taken from grade-A studies and some from grade-C studies, with the aim of illustrating the qualities that distinguish an excellent study from a merely competent one.

It is a useful exercise to study these extracts, taking note of what the examiner praises and the errors some candidates make. This will help you to develop your work using the examples of best practice.

Example 1

What do the contemporary films _American Beauty_* (1999) and _Fight Club_* (1999) show us about the changing role of men in contemporary American society?

■ ■ ■

Grade-A candidate

In recent years, males have been subject to different representations within the media due to changing social and economic climates that are reflecting how men view not only themselves, but also society as a whole. These two films are incredibly different in the presentation of their material, but both films seem to possess similar ideologies.

> _e_ This opening paragraph alone is given full marks for the synoptic element of Module 5. It is an excellent summary of the relevant context for the study that follows.

American Beauty (DreamWorks Pictures) is a film that deconstructs American suburban society, a savage dig at the perfection of normal life that shows how 'normal life' in the American dream is anything but normal. The film is photographed in gloriously sun-washed widescreen; the film's colour is rich and lush in an attempt to show a superficially 'beautiful' environment. This is a clever subversion of traditional representations of the American dream and adds weight to the film. Lester is a 40-something loser stuck in a dead-end job that he despises; to make his mid-life crisis complete, his wife hates him and his daughter holds him in contempt.

> _e_ This passage is written in a commanding style and shows that the candidate has a firm grasp of the subject matter. The film is contextualised in terms of both its institutional and technical background and the cultural frame in which it was produced. The vocabulary is sophisticated and there is a strong sense of the candidate's critical autonomy.

The hero, Jack, in _Fight Club_ seems far more resigned to his fate than Lester in _American Beauty_; his life is joyless but he knows there is little he can do about it. Tyler Durden, over a drink in a bar, makes him realise that what he has is merely 'stuff' and it does not give him basic survival skills. Outside, Tyler surprises Jack by asking him to hit him, behaviour that seems deeply rooted in masculine violence, a strong theme in the film. The fact that Jack starts fighting with Tyler on a regular basis and that it eventually becomes so popular with young men of their age suggests that these young men are intensely frustrated, an ideology that Tyler expresses quite clearly when he says: 'We were raised by television to believe that we'd be millionaires and film gods and rock stars — but we _won't_. And we're learning that fact. And we're very, very pissed off.'

The film seems to blame men's failure in the modern world on two points: consumerism and women.

example

e This closely argued and well-illustrated passage never loses sight of the title's focus.

The films *American Beauty* and *Fight Club* appear to be scathing indictments of modern society, attacking the current representation of males in the films and citing modern society and repression in all its forms as turning every man into a potential self-destroyer.

e There is a slight feeling that a concluding comment in the candidate's own voice should follow this paragraph, but perhaps he/she deliberately leaves the reader musing on the powerful implications of the last point.

Synoptic element (AO1 and AO2): 15

Research element (AO5): 43

Total: 58/60

Example 2

A critical examination of the representation of African-Caribbean men on British television, with reference to *Babyfather*.

■ ■ ■

Grade-A candidate

> *The first point to make is that the title is not a question or a hypothesis and is a little too general. It could be rephrased as something like 'How typical is Babyfather in the representation of African-Caribbean men?' This creates more focus and gives the answer direction.*

A detailed analysis of *Babyfather* will form the focal point of this study, as it will provide the basis of a critical examination of the representation of African-Caribbean males in British television drama.

One of the most relevant concerns in this analysis is the institution of television. This is of importance, as an assessment of the context in which a text is constructed may give some insight as to what the intended or preferred reading was, i.e. what the writer/producer intended to say or portray through the drama in terms of African-Caribbean men and their social habits.

Other contexts, such as the history of representation of this ethnic group, will be investigated as a means of measuring if and how representations of ethnicity on British television have changed in recent years.

This will take place against the background of changes which have taken place in British society over the same period, in particular in response to African-Caribbean immigration. This affects the portrayal of ethnic minorities, given that the media tend to reflect popular attitudes, beliefs and values and also the realities of contemporary life. Representations of minorities could be expected to reflect their growing populations and sociocultural significance and changing attitudes towards them in the majority population. Is the growing population of African-Caribbeans in inner London being appropriately reflected in the drama series *Babyfather*?

> *The candidate makes a clear attempt to place the study in a historical context and address the issue of black stereotypes. The objective of reviewing 'changes which have taken place in British society' seems overly ambitious and perhaps beyond the scope of a 3,000-word text-based study. However, the candidate maintains the focus in the following paragraph.*

If it is true that television is an excellent indicator of the consensus view of society, then this change of attitude should be evident in today's television. The above-mentioned stereotypes of those of African-Caribbean origin in the past should be

example

replaced with more positive images. It would therefore be interesting to note whether or not some of these stereotypes are still evident in a contemporary text such as *Babyfather*.

There is evidence of considerable research (this is apparent throughout the study as well as in the passages above), and the candidate is working towards the chosen text. The rest of the study gives a detailed analysis of the BBC as an institution and a review of the narrative and representations in episodes of *Babyfather*. The conclusion spends time discussing the controversy surrounding the author and his struggle to maintain the integrity of his work and retain some control of storylines to avoid reversion to stereotypes of the black male. This explores the social, political and economic contexts effectively and meets the assessment criteria without detracting from the textual analysis. As a whole, the study is well researched, covers the Key Concepts and has a strong conclusion. It just merits being included in the 51–60 band.

Synoptic element (AO1 and AO2): 10

Research element (AO5): 41

Total: 51/60

Example 3

Does the way in which the news is presented affect how it is perceived and does it create moral panics in its audience?

■ ■ ■

Grade-A candidate

> *e* This is a very specific title but one which does not immediately identify a particular text.

The way in which a news story is presented is of fundamental importance with regard to how it is perceived. Views and opinions are shaped depending on the way events are conveyed and so consequently public reaction is significantly affected.

> *e* This is a clear and deliberate opening statement which sets out the terms of the debate.

With regard to the case of Holly Wells and Jessica Chapman and their brutal murder, news coverage was extensive and unrelenting. Facts, figures, pictures and harrowing real-life accounts of the girls' final moments were all published and broadcast in an attempt to capture public attention and encapsulate the feelings of the nation. The story, and the way it was depicted, provoked public debate about child safety in both the school and the home. Calls to 'name and shame' paedophiles resurfaced; concerns over internet access by children were discussed; vigilantes, witch-hunts and mob rule were all incited in the weeks the story took centre stage. Was all this the consequence of the way the story was presented, and did newspapers and broadcasters serve to encourage this moral panic among their audience, or was it simply the unavoidable result of reporting such horrific events?

> *e* In this strong, well-written opening paragraph the candidate approaches a harrowing and distressing topic in a mature and responsible way. A clear question has emerged which focuses on important media issues relating to sensational journalism and 'moral panic'.

Blanket coverage of all events surrounding the story ensured the case remained in the public eye. All national newspapers dedicated their front pages to the story every day, dating from 4 August until approximately 18 August. It is perhaps worth noting that this high summer period is sometimes called 'the silly season' in media circles, implying that during the summer holidays there is an absence of political news as parliament is in recess and politicians are on holiday. This means that journalists are looking for stories to fill their papers and broadcasts, and in the absence of competition, stories that might not last very long continue to hold the headlines for several days. Tabloids and broadsheets continued to allocate many column inches to the story, ensuring that public debate was inevitable and moral panic took root.

example

> 🖉 The candidate continues authoritatively, outlining the progress of the coverage and relating it to the chief concerns of the title.

John Hartley suggests that 'news photos play a crucial role in the construction of meaning in a story' and this is explicitly evident in the case of Holly Wells and Jessica Chapman. Pictures published showed the girls to be innocent, fun loving and stereotypically ideal children. The image of the two girls beaming, staring out from heavy fringes, dressed in bright red Manchester United T-shirts became iconic. Pictures used by newspapers and broadcasters on a regular basis develop iconic status as they become instantly recognisable by the audience and invoke all the issues relating to the story. The picture released of Myra Hindley is a prime example of iconic photography generated by the reporting of news. The photo was continually re-used and never updated; its depiction of a manic face shadowed by dark lighting made Hindley appear demonic, possibly jeopardising her case and any sympathy that may have been held for her as the victim of her sadistic male partner in the Moors Murder case. The failure to update such a photo ensured that every time the case was mentioned for review, the photo would instantly be called to mind and public hatred was re-evoked.

Similarly, the aforementioned photographs of Holly Wells and Jessica Chapman took on this same iconic status. Instantly recognisable, they began to represent the fading hopes and deep sadness of the country as the search continued for the tragically lost little girls. The pictures ensured the involvement of all families and parents in the concerns for the missing children and helped create a wider panic over issues of paedophilia and child safety.

> 🖉 This is a high standard of debate. The candidate treats a sensitive and disturbing issue with maturity and serious concern. Social and historical contexts are referenced and appropriate theory is engaged with. The candidate goes on to consider Stanley Cohen's seminal work *Folk Devils and Moral Panics* in relation to media coverage and the public's reaction to news reports. Detailed textual references to specific newspaper coverage of the events surrounding the Soham tragedy are included, leading to the crucial contemporary debate about 'trial by media' in relation to the treatment of Huntley and Carr by the press. Drawing the study to a conclusion, the candidate continues:

Perhaps it is true to say that the media encourage 'ghoulish voyeurism'. However, readers and audiences are responsible for buying papers and watching programmes. We do not have to let news merely filter into our consciousness as the simplistic hypodermic theory suggests. On the contrary, we are able to make our own decisions as to whether a story is presented objectively or not. The media play on moral concerns that are already present in our society but remain dormant until hyped up by blanket coverage. However, there can be no doubt that the public's perception of the importance of events is in direct proportion to the amount of coverage they receive in the media.

e This is a sophisticated analysis which touches on media issues of genuine public concern. The candidate shows further awareness of audience theory, and an understanding of how public opinion can be directed and shaped by media coverage of events. There is also recognition of the active audience, making choices and selections from media output, and no attempt to resort to reductionist 'media conspiracy' theories to explain the 'moral panic' phenomenon. Clear evidence of 'critical autonomy', application of Key Concepts and wider contexts all justify a reward in the top band.

Synoptic element (AO1 and AO2): 9

Research element (AO5): 44

Total: 53/60

Example 4

Two months after the twin towers fell, the tabloid press have become less united in the support of allied action in Afghanistan.

■ ■ ■

Grade-A candidate

> *e* As we saw on page 21, the clearly directed title is presented as a statement rather than a question. Would a question have been more appropriate? What really matters is how the candidate's purpose is set out in the opening paragraph.

I will be looking at how two opposing views have emerged concerning the allied action in the 'war on terror' in Afghanistan. What is of particular interest within the split is that a critical battle has emerged between the *Sun* and the *Mirror*. I will analyse 1 week of news articles in the two tabloids concerning the war in Afghanistan. The dates of the investigation will be between 12 November 2001 and 17 November 2001. The initial aim will be to identify a clear and distinctive contrast in each newspaper's perception of the war and to distinguish the many factors involved in bringing about this difference of opinion concerning the allied action.

I have chosen to work around the particular week of 12 November 2001 to 17 November 2001 so that the attitudes and ideologies of each newspaper before and after the liberation of Kabul will be apparent.

> *e* A clearly defined sense of purpose and a specific range of focused texts emerges from this paragraph. The candidate continues in this manner with a brief analysis of the ideological positioning of the *Sun* and *Mirror*, contextualising the study before engaging in a more detailed textual analysis.

On Monday 12 November 2001, the *Sun* presented the Northern Alliance victories with the headline, 'We rule half the country'. The word 'we' instantly links the Northern Alliance with the allied nations, that is with Britain and America. This also promotes a sense of patriotism and nationalism among the readers. The success of the Northern Alliance is spread across two pages, with the 'war on terror' update on the left corner of page 6 alongside the story of their progress and a diagram to support the material. The war on terror update suggests that the *Sun* has been closely watching the progress of the war with its own journalist actually present in Afghanistan. This connotes the paper's interactive support for the conflict and the language used further emphasises this, describing the Alliance's assault as 'inflicting shattering defeats on the Taliban' and embellishing the article with the emboldened words: 'Advancing...Reached... Overrun...Smashed'.

> *e* The candidate has embarked on a detailed textual analysis, making evaluation an intrinsic part of the process. In the next paragraph the approach of the *Mirror* is contrasted with that of the *Sun*.

'Prisoners skinned alive, women raped, victims tortured...should we call these killers our friends?' Contrary to the *Sun's* glamorous portrayal of the Northern Alliance, the *Mirror* reader is presented with a completely different perception. There is a medium close-up picture of General Abdul Rashid Dostum, who is described in the anchoring text as the 'feared leader'. To label a man 'feared' during wartime would definitely raise eyebrows about his actions and this is what the journalist probably intends. The general is pictured in his uniform with his hands clenched, almost suggesting he is planning or scheming as his eyes contract to connote an image of evil. His moustache is unkempt and he is looking away from the cameras, suggesting connotations of shame. The picture has been chosen to support the *Mirror's* story, with the emphasis on the 'feared leader' suggesting that this is not a person we can sympathise with or see as a hero. The *Mirror* has always been against the western armies' link with the Northern Alliance and this is reflected in the treatment of this article.

e The candidate continues the close analysis of specific material, highlighting the differences between the two newspapers.

This extract shows that the *Sun* prides itself on its stance of consistent support and is blatantly criticising those who were against the conflict. 'The wobblers should hang their heads in shame' and again 'Shame of the traitors, wrong, wrong, wrong...the fools who said the allies faced disaster.' The article is critical of many newspapers, but the criticism of the *Mirror* is apparent: 'our so-called rival has tried to cover itself in glory — trumpeting its coverage as "in-depth". In fact, what the *Mirror* has done is nothing short of treachery.' The rivalry between the two papers could be said to be distorting their coverage of these important world events.

e Having used detailed textual references to explore the rivalry between the two newspapers, the candidate goes on to discuss their ideological positioning in relation to New Labour and the Bush presidency. Later in the study there are references to Galtung and Ruge and 'news values' theory and institutional factors affecting the newspapers' stances. The key to the success of this piece is the clearly focused textual analysis and a high standard of commentary. Overall, the candidate demonstrates an awareness of wider contextual factors and the Key Concepts throughout. The title's assertion is fully justified in the body of the essay. This study is a solid grade A.

Synoptic element (AO1 and AO2): 9

Research element (AO5): 45

Total: 54/60

Example 5

How successful was the marketing campaign for _Spider-Man_ (2002)?

■ ■ ■

Grade-C candidate

> *e* Questions of the 'how successful was' variety are discouraged because they usually lead to an uncritical review of the history of the campaign behind a successful media product. The fact that the product was successful means that the campaign must have been successful, so the short answer to the above question is 'very'. A more probing question might be 'In what ways did the marketing campaign for _Spider-Man_ contribute to its success?'

Comic book heroes make an attractive prospect for filmmakers and studios. They have a wide fan base that almost, except in the most incompetent of cases, guarantee box office success. Following hot on the heels of _Superman_ (1978), _Batman & Robin_ (1997) and _X-Men_ (2000) came _Spider-Man_, in April 2002. As well as a wide fan base, they also encapsulate the American virtues of decency, hard work and goodness pitted against some foul and usually disabled villain.

> *e* The opening paragraph makes a fair shot at summarising the area of study, but _Spider-Man_ is scarcely 'hot on the heels' of the other comic book movies. The syntax of the whole paragraph is, at best, inelegant. The candidate does not make a totally fluent or convincing first impression.

The values and ideology within the film are good versus evil, Spider-Man is fighting for the good of the public, and the Green Goblin is for fighting for evil and crime. Light and dark is also present in the film, Spider-Man is fighting for good, a connotation of which is light, and the Green Goblin fighting for evil, darkness is a connotation of evil, death, etc. The film fits in with today's society through the use of values and ideology. The American society is represented by the side fighting for good, it shows the American society as hardworking, decent people.

> *e* The original spelling, punctuation and syntax are retained to illustrate the detrimental effect they have on what the candidate is trying to say. This passage is typical of the body of the essay: fairly descriptive and basic. Good and evil are binary opposites — a missed opportunity to mention Levi-Strauss and narrative theory. They also represent simplistic ideological positions which are easy for a young (or not so young) audience to relate to and adopt. There is no critical analysis or comment on the simplistic version of morality being offered by the film, and an opportunity to demonstrate critical autonomy and a deeper awareness of the issues is lost. The candidate's thinking comes across as woolly. How exactly does the film 'fit in with today's society through the use of values and ideology'?

The essay's attempts to introduce theory are clumsy and artificial. For example:

The theories tied in with the film are the hypodermic model, reception analysis, and Marxism. The hypodermic model is the idea that mass media are so powerful that they can inject their 'message' into their audience, in other words they believe that the makers of media messages can get the audience to do what they want them to do. Serious theorists have discredited the hypodermic model. In the case of *Spider-Man* the media message is injected to make people watch the film, the syringe is represented by the marketing campaign. And the audience represents the patient.

✎ Little advantage is gained by discussing the hypodermic theory at this point. There is no further application of theory to the film: the next paragraph discusses age and the viewing practices of different age groups. The essay is disjointed and the above paragraph seems to be included merely to cover a perceived need to make some reference to theory. This occurs again with a gesture towards discussing Marxism.

The Marxist theory was more dominantly used in the mid-1960s to the mid-1980s, although it is still used by theorists in media research. The theory suggests that the dominant social class rule is used in the media. In today's society the theory concentrates on the dominant gender, race and country that rules what the media do.

✎ There is little justification for introducing this reference to Marxism, as it does not help to answer the question, and the passage is poorly written. The essay continues with details of *Spider-Man* websites and their success, and then digresses to a history of superhero films and the development of computer-generated imagery. It concludes by citing the amounts earned by the film as justification for the claim that the marketing campaign was a success.

The weakness of the title makes it difficult for the candidate to engage in analytical debate. However, there is enough merit in the work overall to justify a mark in the 31–40 range.

Synoptic element (AO1 and AO2): 8

Research element (AO5): 28

Total: 36/60

Example 6

How does Mercedes-Benz's contemporary 'Lucky Star' advertisement embody the ideology of the brand?

■ ■ ■

Grade-C candidate

> *e* This is a clear question, even a demanding one. 'Ideology of the brand' sounds an elusive concept, but in the right hands this could be promising. The text studied will of course be the advertisement, but there is a danger that what follows may be more about the car and Mercedes than the media product.

The concept of branding in the car industry evolved due to the primitive technology applied to the manufacture of the products in the early days of the industry. Companies selected their target market because they did not have the resources available to them to meet the requirements of all consumers. Brands were developed on the strength of their products as each company specifically targeted different sections of society, therefore creating a class system within the industry.

> *e* Although competent, the opening discussion only deals with branding. What is the study actually going to be about?

In this essay I will focus on the fortunes of Mercedes-Benz in the marketing of its products. Mercedes has established an elite brand since its creation in 1926 through the continuous production of safe, reliable, high-performance, luxury motorcars. Mercedes vehicles maintain a 'better than the rest' image despite the fact that many economy class cars can now also claim to be just as safe, reliable, luxurious and high performance at half the price of a Mercedes.

> *e* This is interesting enough, but the candidate is supposed to be writing a media studies essay, not a history of Mercedes-Benz. The information may have been included by way of background contextualising, but it remains to be seen whether there will be a focused analysis of media products.

There is also competition from other luxury class cars, such as the rival German brand BMW and the former British brand Jaguar. Mercedes has to keep one step ahead of these 'executive' brands because for every BMW or Jaguar sold, a Mercedes has not been. It must be seen to be the market leader in this field and can only achieve this through brand promotion.

> *e* This is starting to read more like a business studies essay than a media studies one. What follows is an account of the Lucky Star campaign, which reads like an advertising agency release, without any real application of media Key Concepts or media perspectives.

Mercedes wanted the advert to be entertaining, branded and relevant. According to Casper Thykier, Director of Campbell, Doyle, Dye, the advertising agency responsible for the promotion, 'We had to communicate the specialism of the Mercedes brand and apply the quality of the car to the quality of the commercial' (*The Making of Lucky Star*, television documentary).

 This anchors the study firmly in the documentary cited and the candidate goes on to describe the content of the advertisement in some detail.

The second scene represented is a space scene. The sky is black and littered with stars, you can see shots of planets, mainly earth, the sun and a lunar landscape. There are shots of planets aligning; this has huge astrological connotations with the concept of luck. These space scenes represent the technological advancements of the human race and the universal appeal of the Mercedes car brand. The next location is the stock market. This representation is conveyed by the design of the office; it is full of desks, which have computers, television monitors and telephones. This is a high-powered and competitive business environment where success is often signified by Mercedes ownership. Salaries can be very high and the activity is often portrayed in the media as exciting but cut-throat and hazardous (e.g. the 1980s movie *Wall Street* with Michael Douglas). It also acts as a representation of the target audience's work place; stereotypical Mercedes owners hold high positions at big businesses and are therefore very familiar with the workings of the stock market, as the state of the economy has huge implications on the success of their corporation.

 This scene-by-scene deconstruction of the advertisement helps to position the candidate in relation to the subject and the Key Concept of representation. Some attempt is made to include social, historical and economic contextual factors. Analysis of the 'ideology' of the brand is on a competent level. Having worked through the scenes, the candidate goes on to discuss representation and audiences in the following terms:

The representation of both men and women in this trailer appears to be very uneven. The number of males far exceeds the number of females, with 7 out of the 10 main characters being men. The male characters all appear to be between the age of 30 to 50 while all the women appear to be between the age of 18 to 29. This would indicate that the advert is aimed at men between the ages of 30 to 50 and the presence of the female gender is to appeal to what is known in media terms as the 'male gaze'. The women represent potentially desirable partners for the older, 'successful' Mercedes owner, and in spite of the sophistication of the product the appeal is at a fairly basic psychological level: 'Buy a Mercedes and win the girl' — a proposition proven to be effective with males in this age bracket. This well-tried and 'sexist' approach confirms that aspiring, middle-aged males are the prime target audience for the advert.

 The candidate makes a good point about representation in terms of gender balance and age, with speculation as to the market for the advert. The reference to 'male gaze' suggests understanding of relevant theoretical perspectives on the

representation of women for male audiences and demonstrates some awareness of wider social contextual issues.

This advertisement turned out to be very successful for Mercedes; it managed to draw huge demand for the SL class, forcing Mercedes to compile a waiting list for the product. It also partly contributed to Mercedes's twelfth position in the list of the 'Top 100 Global Brands'. It is very important for brands like Mercedes that they maintain a distance between themselves and rivals, constantly emphasising their elite status as a 'unique selling point'. Creating and maintaining a mystique around the brand plays a vital part in sustaining its market position. Brands such as Mercedes play an important part in defining 'lifestyle' choices in advanced capitalist societies and are used by individuals as measures of their achievements and identity. It is just as important for the company that Mercedes cars remain a coveted and desired product for the many who cannot afford them, and advertisements of this kind are designed to maintain that position.

Overall, this study meets the criteria for a mark in the range 31–40. There is a descriptive, scene-by-scene account with competent to good evaluation and focus. Understanding and development of the Key Concepts, particularly representation, are sound and there is some evidence of wider application. The candidate focuses on the topic, but relies too heavily on one source text — the documentary. There is limited reference to media theory and only one media textbook is referred to in the bibliography. However, the candidate tries to bring in wider social, political, historical and economic contexts. The piece is clear and well organised and offers a critical account and evaluation of the advertisement. The lack of further development in the work and the partial exploration of ideas and concepts justifies a final mark of 33.

Synoptic element (AO1 and AO2): 8

Research element (AO5): 25

Total: 33/60

Example 7

Media publicity has built up *Kabhi Khushi Kabhi Gham* (*K3G*) to be the most successful Bollywood film.

■ ■ ■

Grade-C candidate

e As was discussed on page 22, this title lacks a critical or discursive dimension. The candidate is likely to produce a study based on demonstrating the truth of the assertion rather than engaging in an investigation or discursive analysis.

With the rise of Bollywood movies entering the British film charts, it is difficult to ignore the fact that such films are becoming more recognised and successful throughout the world and are reaching a much wider audience than they did 10 years ago. For this reason Bollywood has become of great media interest and my essay will be looking at the release of a major Bollywood film, *Kabhi Khushi Kabhi Gham*, also known as *K3G*, through television advertisements and the printed press, such as magazines and newspapers and posters, from the time that music was released in August 2001 till the film release in December 2001.

e This is a fair opening paragraph but one that seems to point towards a descriptive review of the film's release and reception. It is unclear how the study will develop.

Kabhi Khushi Kabhi Gham was released on 14 December 2001 and its outcome was eagerly awaited. It reached number 3 in the UK box office after just 2 weeks of release, coming number 3 after *Harry Potter* and *The Lord of the Rings*. The British audience was given a taster into the making of the film in July 2001 when Ruby Wax did a documentary on Bollywood and followed the making of *K3G*. Since then the audience had been awaiting the release of the movie. Already the film was trying to reach a wider audience than just the Asians in Britain, namely the non-Asians who may have an interest in Bollywood, and the fact that it was shown on mainstream television at a prime time of 10 p.m. demonstrated this. Ruby Wax spoke positively of the film and showed the actors in a positive light. The documentary emphasised the fact that the film was India's most expensive extravaganza in the last decade and was too big to be ignored.

e The study is developing a narrative voice in describing publicity for the film. Had the title been given a questioning focus, the candidate would have been directed towards a more analytical approach. As the study develops it becomes clear that the candidate has done a great deal of research on the film.

Amitabh Bachcham is one of the most well-known Bollywood actors. He also has a waxwork model in London's Madame Tussaud's. His screen performances, combined with his wife Hrithik Roshan, were a hit in the early 1970s and 1980s. Their collaboration in *K3G* came after an 18-year gap. This fact was used by the media to appeal to

the older generation of the over 35s who had enjoyed watching the couple on screen in the 1970s and 1980s. The director also used this pair to represent the traditional Indian parents as they are of the older generation and older parents of around 40 and above would be able to relate to them.

> *ℓ* The candidate demonstrates how the film was constructed to appeal to a wide audience and touches on issues of representation which could have been developed had there been more direction in the title. The study continues with detailed descriptions of media publicity for the film and the appeal of different actors to different elements of the audience. Once again, representation is touched on in explaining the publicity posters:

The advertising of *K3G* shows the film to be a family-orientated one. The slogan 'It's all about loving your parents' featured on all posters, and the advertisements tell the audience what the film is about without giving away the storyline. It indicates that the film is suitable for all the family to enjoy and will have a lot of strong, traditional, Indian family values. The posters, CD covers, article and magazine advertisements all show a family portrait. The actors and actresses are all smiling and look like a happy family. They show an Indian family that consists of a traditional mother, father, sons and daughters-in-law. Two older women are wearing traditional saris and have a red line in their middle parting on their foreheads along with the black-beaded necklaces. This indicates that they are married Indian women and underlines the traditional values of the film.

> *ℓ* This is another largely descriptive passage, but the candidate attempts to analyse and explain the representations described. The study continues in this manner with descriptions of a trailer and explanations of how the representations might appeal to an Indian audience. Further paragraphs explain the music score and how this was released before the film to stimulate interest, and also how the *mise-en-scène* and narrative treatment appeal to an audience. The study is well documented and thorough for its type. It has been included because it represents an approach often adopted by candidates. Had it been more analytical, perhaps including a comparative analysis of more than one film or a question relating to the relevance of traditional family representations for young Asians in Britain, the study could have been awarded a higher grade. The grade given was a low C, largely because of the descriptive and unchallenging nature of the content.

Synoptic element (AO1 and AO2): 6

Research element (AO5): 26

Total: 32/60